EASY PIANO

# MUSIC FROM MINECRAFT

T0086979

ISBN 978-1-70514-219-6

7777 W. BLUEMOUND RD. P.O. BOX 13819 MILWAUKEE, WI 53213

Visit Hal Leonard Online at
**www.halleonard.com**

Contact us:
**Hal Leonard**
7777 West Bluemound Road
Milwaukee, WI 53213
Email: info@halleonard.com

In Europe, contact:
**Hal Leonard Europe Limited**
42 Wigmore Street
Marylebone, London, W1U 2RN
Email: info@halleonardeurope.com

In Australia, contact:
**Hal Leonard Australia Pty. Ltd.**
4 Lentara Court
Cheltenham, Victoria, 3192 Australia
Email: info@halleonard.com.au

# ALPHA
### from MINECRAFT: VOLUME BETA

By DANIEL ROSENFELD

**Moderately**

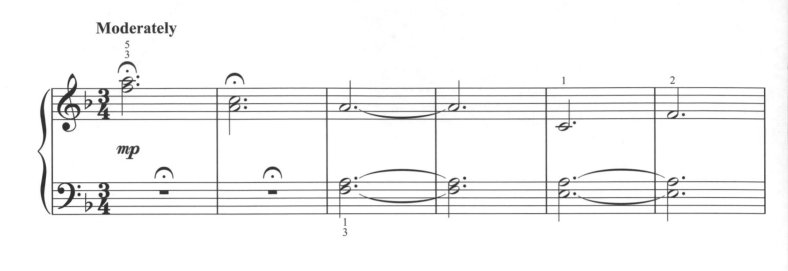

**Slower**

*rit.*

**Faster**

**Slowly**   **Moderately fast**

# ARIA MATH

## from MINECRAFT: VOLUME BETA

By DANIEL ROSENFELD

# CAT
## from MINECRAFT: VOLUME ALPHA

By DANIEL ROSENFELD

**Moderately**

# CLARK
## from MINECRAFT: VOLUME ALPHA

By DANIEL ROSENFELD

**Moderately slow, freely**

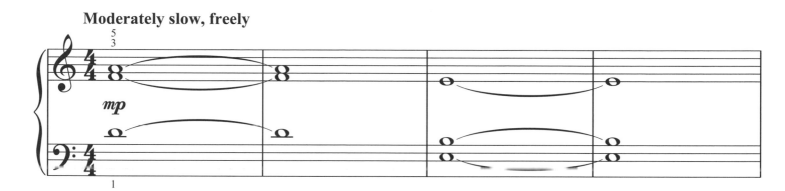

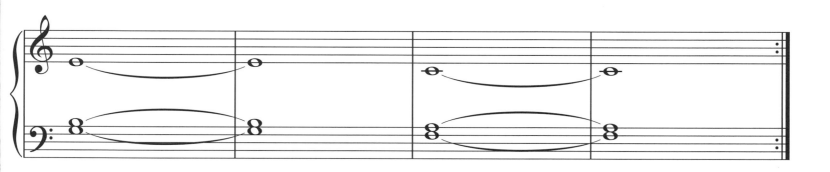

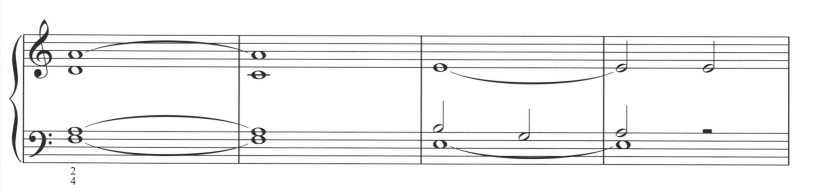

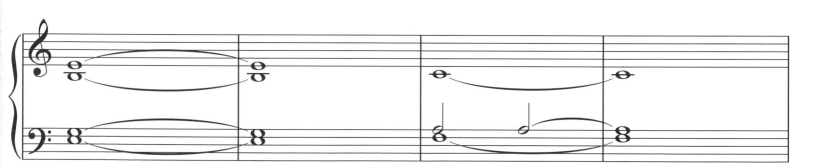

# CHIRP
## from MINECRAFT: VOLUME BETA

By DANIEL ROSENFELD

**Moderately fast**

# DANNY
## from MINECRAFT: VOLUME ALPHA

By DANIEL ROSENFELD

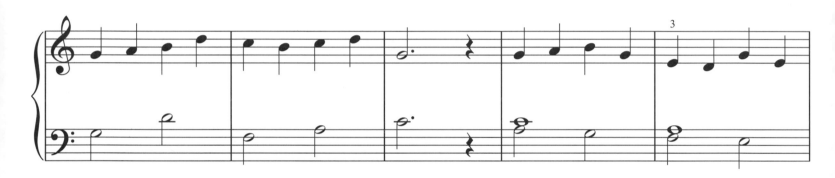

*a tempo*

# DRY HANDS
## from MINECRAFT: VOLUME ALPHA

By DANIEL ROSENFELD

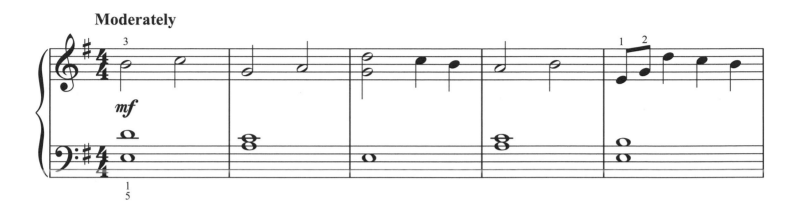

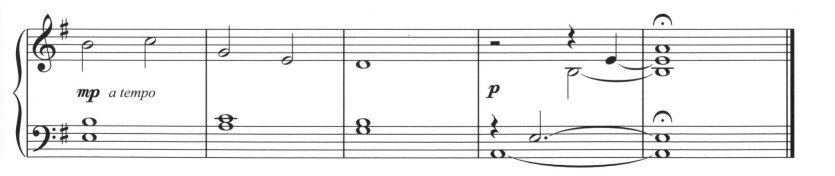

# DOOR
## from MINECRAFT: VOLUME ALPHA

By DANIEL ROSENFELD

**Moderately**

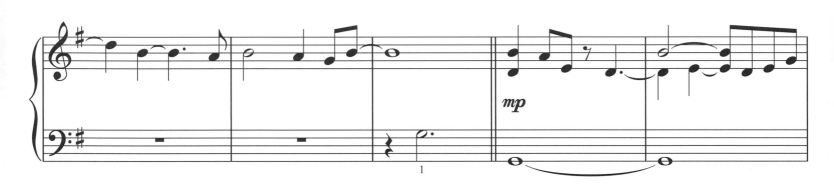

# FAR
## from MINECRAFT: VOLUME BETA

By DANIEL ROSENFELD

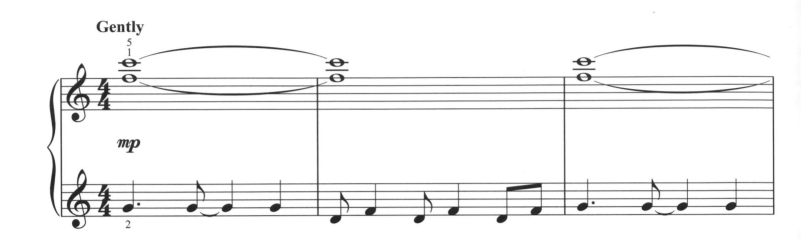

# HAGGSTROM
## from MINECRAFT: VOLUME ALPHA

By DANIEL ROSENFELD

# LIVING MICE
## from MINECRAFT: VOLUME ALPHA

By DANIEL ROSENFELD

*rit.*

# MELLOHI
## from MINECRAFT: VOLUME BETA

By DANIEL ROSENFELD

# MICE ON VENUS
## from MINECRAFT: VOLUME ALPHA

By DANIEL ROSENFELD

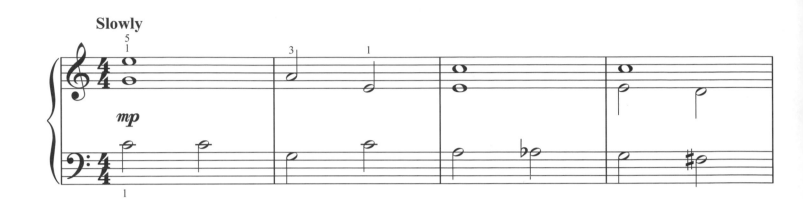

Moderately

# MINECRAFT
## from MINECRAFT: VOLUME ALPHA

By DANIEL ROSENFELD

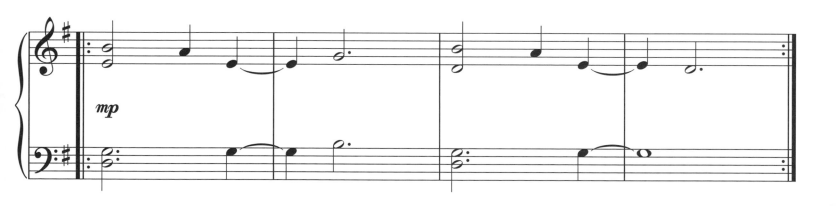

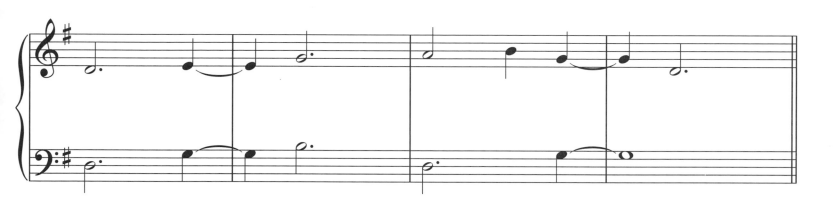

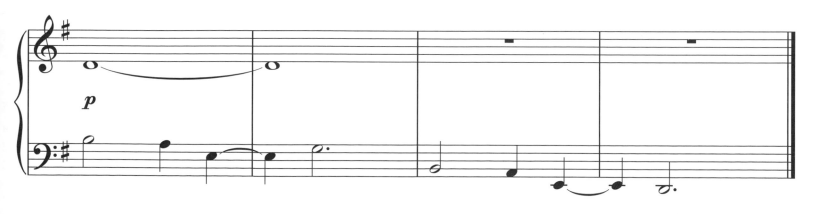

# MOOG CITY
## from MINECRAFT: VOLUME ALPHA

By DANIEL ROSENFELD

**Moderately**

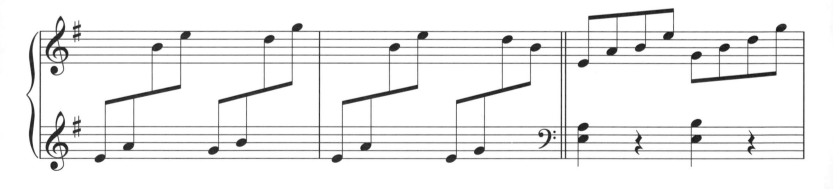

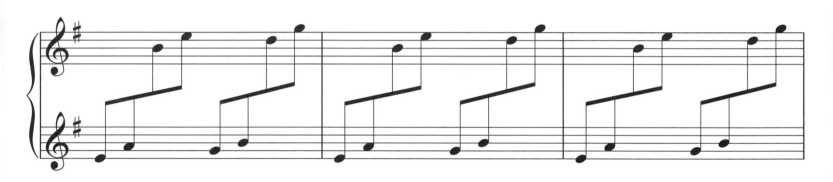

# MUTATION
## from MINECRAFT: VOLUME BETA

By DANIEL ROSENFELD

**Moderately**

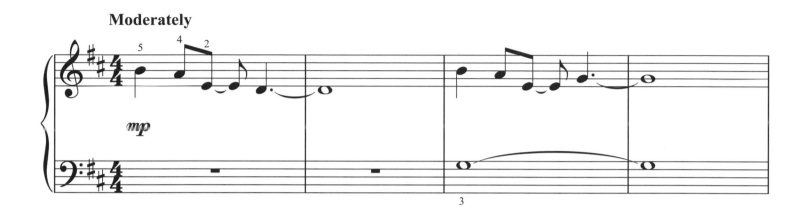

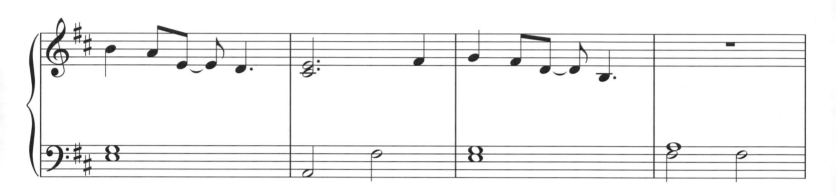

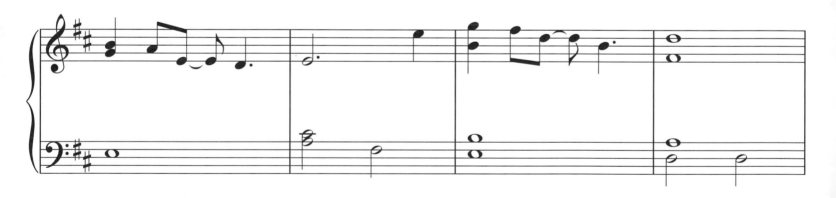

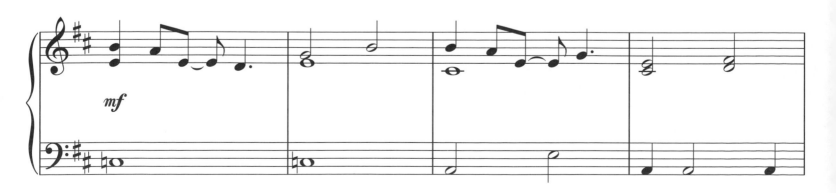

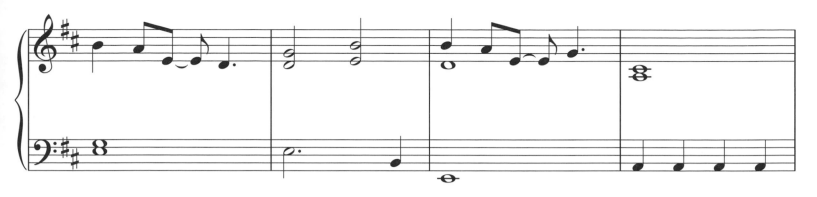

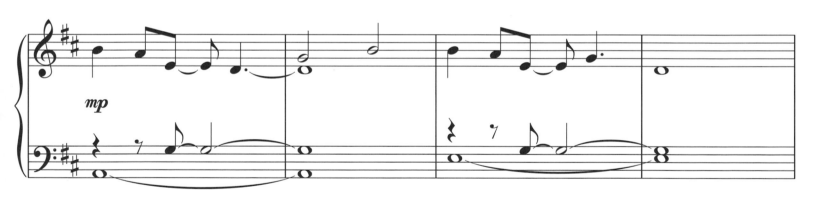

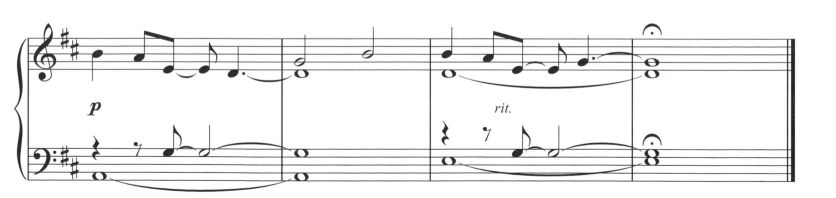

# STAL
## from MINECRAFT: VOLUME BETA

By DANIEL ROSENFELD

# SWEDEN
## from MINECRAFT: VOLUME ALPHA

By DANIEL ROSENFELD

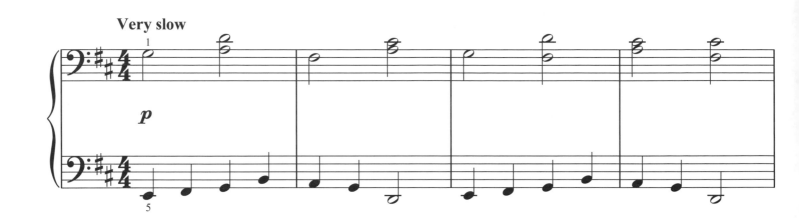

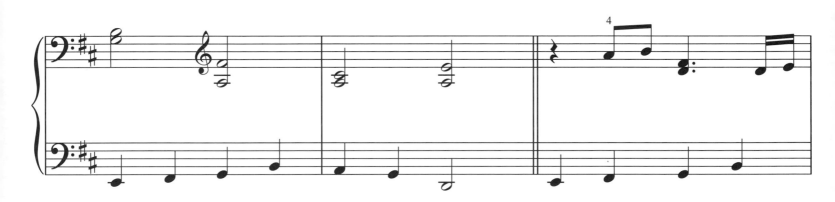

# WET HANDS
## from MINECRAFT: VOLUME ALPHA

By DANIEL ROSENFELD

**Moderately slow**

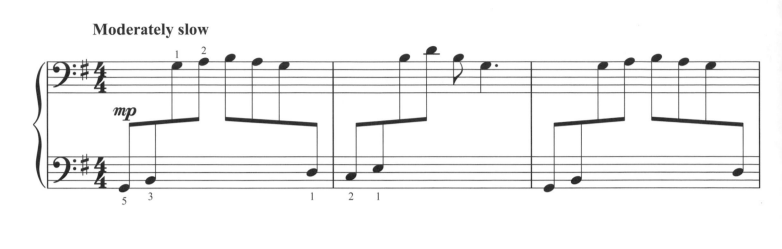

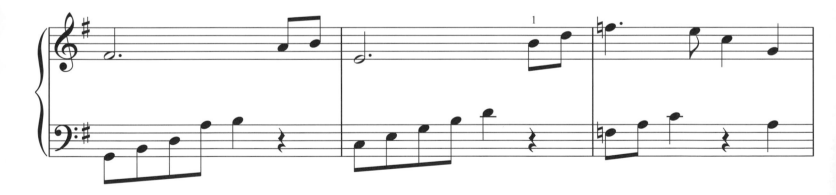

# SUBWOOFER LULLABY

## from MINECRAFT: VOLUME ALPHA

By DANIEL ROSENFELD

**Moderately slow**

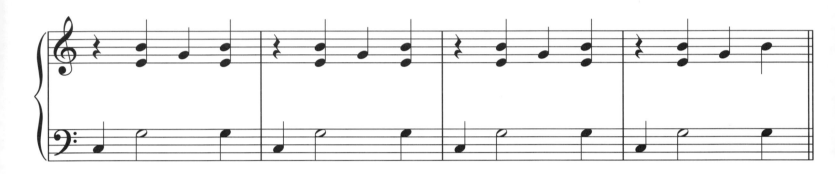

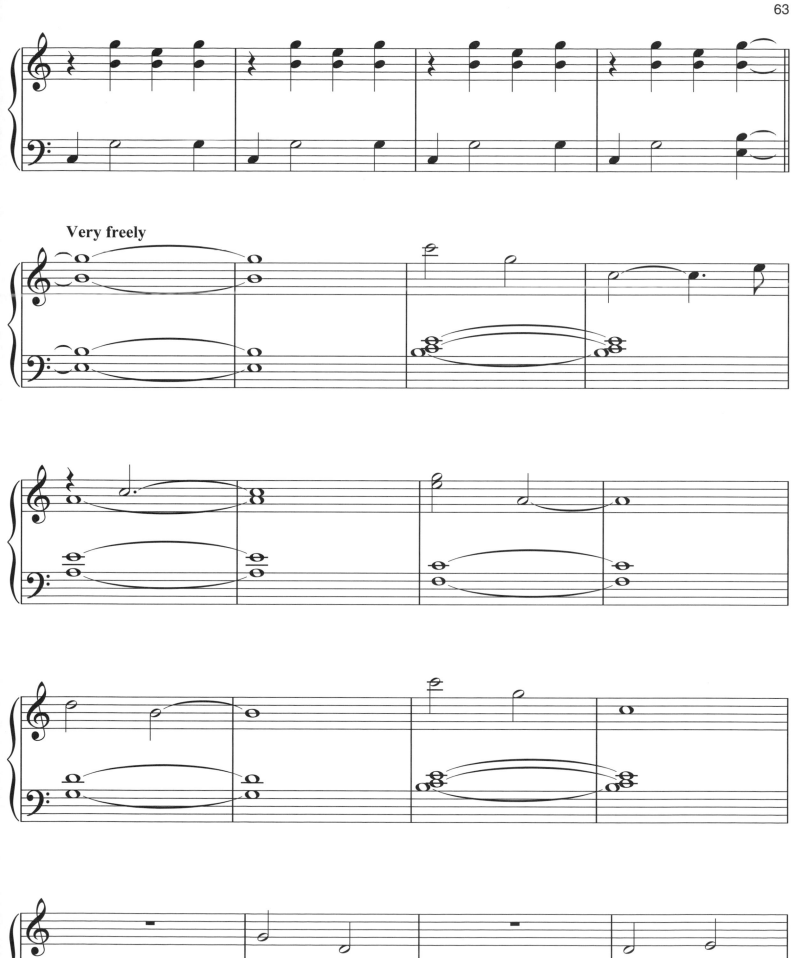

**Very freely**